Sara Swan Miller

Rodents

From Mice to Muskrats

DISCARDED

Franklin Watts - A Division of Grolier Publishing
New York • London • Hong Kong • Sydney • Danbury, Connecticut

For Lani Miller, in hopes you will learn to love them

Photographs ©: Animals Animals: 17 (Raymond A. Mendez); BBC Natural History Unit: 5 bottom right (Andrew Cooper), 19 (Jeff Foott), 1 (Dietmar Nill), 23, 29 (Warwick Sloss), 5 top right, 7, 21 (Artur Talbor); International Stock Photo: 41 (Ron Sanford); Photo Researchers: 33 (Nick Bergkessel), 42 bottom (Stephen Dalton), 43 (Francois Gohier), 15 (Tom McHugh), 39 (Leonard Lee Rue, III); Visuals Unlimited: 35 (Gerard & Buff Corsi), cover, 31 (John Gerlach), 25 (Parke H. John, Jr.), 13 (Joe McDonald), 40 (Arthur Morris), 6 (Glenn Oliver); The Wildlife Collection: 37 (Bob Bennett), 27 (Michael Francis), 42 top (Robert Lankinen), 5 bottom left (Charles Melton), 5 top left (Tom Vezo).

Illustrations by Jose Gonzales and Steve Savage

Visit Franklin Watts on the Internet at:
http://publishing.grolier.com

Library of Congress Cataloging-in-Publication Data

Miller, Sara Swan.
Rodents: from mice to muskrats / Sara Swan Miller.
    p. cm. — (Animals in order)
    Includes bibliographical references and index.
    Summary: A general overview of rodents, including a description of fourteen species and recommendations for observing them.
    ISBN 0-531-11488-0 (lib.bdg.)   0-531-15920-5 (pbk.)
    1. Rodents—Juvenile literature. 2. Rodents—Classification—Juvenile literature.
[1. Rodents.]   I. Title.   II. Series.
QL737.R6M55   1998
599.35—dc21
                                                    97-24034
                                                    CIP
                                                    AC

Contents

How Do You Know It's a Rodent?

Everyone knows what a rodent is, or do they? If someone asked you to describe a rodent, what would you say? You would probably think of a mouse scurrying across the floor. Or maybe you would picture a rat racing through a sewer. Rodents are small, furry animals that run quickly about, right? Not always!

Not all small, quick, and furry animals are rodents. And not all rodents are small—or quick. Some, like porcupines, are large and rather slow.

Three of the four animals on the next page belong to a special group called the rodents. The fourth animal is not a rodent. Can you guess which ones are rodents?

Woodchuck

Shrew

Squirrel

Vole

Traits of a Rodent

The vole, the squirrel, and the woodchuck are all rodents, but the shrew is not. Was that what you guessed?

The best way to decide whether an animal is a rodent is by looking at its teeth. A rodent has two front teeth—called *incisors*—that look like little chisels. The next three teeth that most other *mammals* have are missing in rodents, so there is a gap between their incisors and their *cheek teeth*. Most rodents nip and gnaw with their incisors and chew with their cheek teeth.

The front of each incisor is coated with a layer of hard material called enamel, but the back is soft. When a rodent gnaws, the back of its incisors wears down faster than the front. That keeps its incisors very sharp. You might think rodents would wear down their incisors with all the gnawing they do, but the incisors grow constantly, so they never wear down.

Rodents come in all sizes—small, medium, and large. A white-footed mouse weighs less than 1 ounce (28 g). A woodchuck weighs about 10 pounds (4.5 kg). A beaver can weigh up to 100 pounds (45 kg)!

Different kinds of rodents eat different

Muskrat skull

Forest dormouse

kinds of foods. Some eat mostly green plants, while others gnaw on tree bark. Still others like seeds and nuts best. Many small rodents eat insects. A few rodents, such as squirrels, also eat eggs or young birds.

Rodents live all over the world, except in Antarctica. They can be found in just about every kind of *habitat*.

The Order of Living Things

A tiger has more in common with a house cat than with a daisy. A scorpion is more like a butterfly than a jellyfish. Scientists arrange living things into groups based on how they look and how they act. A tiger and a house cat belong to the same group, but a daisy belongs to a different group.

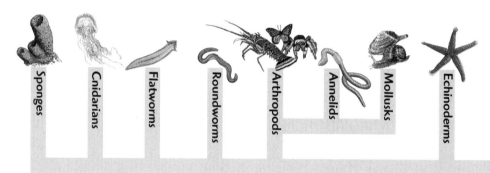

Sponges · Cnidarians · Flatworms · Roundworms · Arthropods · Annelids · Mollusks · Echinoderms

Animals

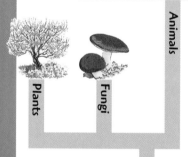

Plants

Fungi

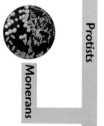

Monerans

Protists

All living things can be placed in one of five groups called *kingdoms:* the plant kingdom, the animal kingdom, the *fungus* kingdom, the moneran kingdom, or the protist kingdom. You can probably name many of the creatures in the plant and animal kingdoms. The fungus kingdom includes mushrooms, yeasts, and molds. The moneran and protist kingdoms contain thousands of living things that are too small to see without a microscope.

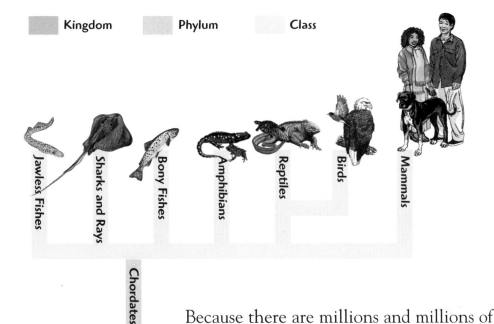

Kingdom | Phylum | Class

Jawless Fishes
Sharks and Rays
Bony Fishes
Amphibians
Reptiles
Birds
Mammals
Chordates

Because there are millions and millions of living things on Earth, some of the members of one kingdom may not seem all that similar. The animal kingdom includes creatures as different as tarantulas and trout, jellyfish and jaguars, salamanders and sparrows, elephants and earthworms.

To show that an elephant is more like a jaguar than an earthworm, scientists further separate the creatures in each kingdom into more specific groups. The animal kingdom can be divided into nine *phyla*. Humans belong to the chordate phylum. All chordates have a backbone.

Each phylum can be subdivided into many *classes*. Humans, mice, and elephants all belong to the mammal class. Each class can be further divided into *orders*; orders into *families*, families into *genera*, and genera into *species*. All of the members of a species are very similar.

How Rodents Fit In

You can probably guess that the rodents belong to the animal kingdom. They have much more in common with snakes and sparrows than with maple trees and morning glories.

Rodents belong to the chordate phylum. Almost all chordates have a backbone and a skeleton. Can you think of other chordates? Examples include elephants, mice, snakes, birds, fish, and whales.

The chordate phylum can be divided into a number of classes. Rodents belong to the mammal class. Elephants, humans, dogs, and cats are all mammals.

There are seventeen different orders of mammals. The rodents make up one of these orders. The scientific name for this order is rodentia, which means "gnawers." As you learned earlier, all rodents have chisel-like incisors that are perfect for gnawing.

The rodents can be divided into a number of different families and genera. There are more than 2,000 different species of rodents. That's almost as many species as all the other orders of mammals combined! You will learn more about some of the rodents in this book.

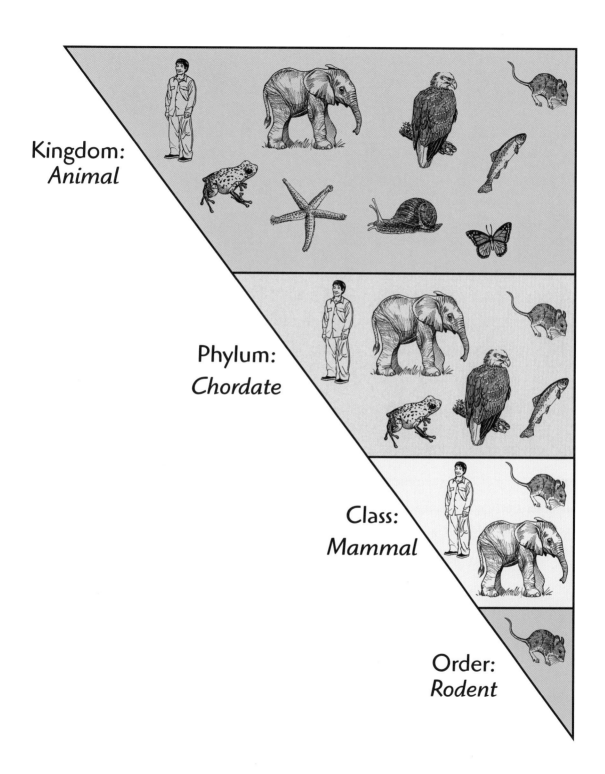

Kingdom:
Animal

Phylum:
Chordate

Class:
Mammal

Order:
Rodent

Marmots

FAMILY: Sciuridae
COMMON EXAMPLE: Woodchuck
GENUS AND SPECIES: *Marmota monax*
SIZE: 20 to 27 inches (51 to 69 cm);
    5 to 10 pounds (2 to 4 kg)

Have you ever come upon a woodchuck nibbling on grassy plants in a field? Every few seconds it sits up and looks around. It has to be very careful because it has many enemies. If a woodchuck sees a *predator*, it lets out a shrill whistle and waddles toward its *burrow* as fast as it can.

Woodchucks, which are sometimes called groundhogs, are expert diggers. Each one digs a large underground burrow with one main entrance and several emergency holes. The main entrance is usually surrounded by a mound of soil and stones. The emergency holes are much harder to spot.

A woodchuck's network of underground tunnels may be up to 30 feet (9 m) long and more than 5 feet (1.5 m) deep. Many little rooms are built off the main tunnel. The sleeping rooms have cozy nests lined with grass. Other rooms are used as toilets.

Woodchucks spend the summer months eating and eating, so they can store up fat for winter. In the fall, each woodchuck digs a winter den, crawls inside, and curls up in a ball. It will not come out for 6 months.

When a woodchuck *hibernates*, its body temperature and heart rate drop so that its stored fat will last longer. Even so, the wood-chuck is scrawny and very hungry by spring. When it comes out of its den, the woodchuck eats every plant in sight!

Voles

FAMILY: Cricetidae
COMMON EXAMPLE: Meadow vole
GENUS AND SPECIES: *Microtus pennsylvanicus*
SIZE: 5 to 7 inches (12 to 18 cm);
   1 to 2 ounces (28 to 56 g)

Just after the snow has melted, have you ever noticed trails about the size of a garden hose running through short grass? These trails tell you that meadow voles have been busy feeding on seeds and roots all winter. They're busy munching away the rest of the year, too—day and night. A meadow vole can eat as much as it weighs in just 24 hours. How much do you weigh? Can you imagine eating that many pounds of food every day?

Voles often dig tunnels just below the soil. Sometimes their tunnels lead to a garden. In early spring, they grab young plants by the roots and drag them into their tunnel. All that's left is a round hole in the ground.

Meadow voles make strong little nests of dried grass and raise *litter* after litter of young voles. A female can give birth to seventeen litters in a single year. There are usually three to five babies in a litter, and females are ready to start having babies when they are just 3 weeks old. So how many baby voles can one mother produce in a year? Try to do the math. Imagine how many voles there would be in the world if lots of other animals didn't love vole meat!

Pocket Gophers

FAMILY: Geomyidae
COMMON EXAMPLE: Southeastern pocket gopher
GENUS AND SPECIES: *Geomys pinetis*
SIZE: 9 to 12 inches (23 to 30 cm); 8 to 15 ounces (227 to 425 g)

Pocket gophers spend most of their time underground, so we don't see them very often. But we can see the mounds of dirt they pile up at the entrances of their burrows. Pocket gophers are constantly working to make their burrows bigger. They loosen dirt with their strong incisors and then push it aside with their front paws. Every now and then, a gopher pushes the dirt out of the tunnel with its head and feet. Gophers are sort of like little, furry bulldozers.

In the part of the burrow near the surface, pocket gophers cut the roots of young plants and pull them underground. They stuff the food into fur-lined pockets in their cheeks and carry it to storerooms deeper underground.

Pocket gophers live alone. They spend time with other gophers only during mating. Unlike most rodents, pocket gophers have just one or two litters of two to six babies a year. Gophers have fewer young than other rodents because their only natural enemy is the gopher snake, which often slithers into their burrows looking for a nice gopher dinner.

17

Prairie Dogs

FAMILY: Sciuridae
COMMON EXAMPLE: Black-tailed prairie dog
GENUS AND SPECIES: *Cynomys ludovicianus*
SIZE: 14 to 17 inches (36 to 43 cm);
2 to 3 pounds (1 to 1.3 kg)

Prairie dogs live together in huge "towns." A prairie-dog town is a series of large underground burrows linked by tunnels. One prairie-dog town—in Texas—was an incredible 250 miles (400 km) long and 100 miles (160 km) wide!

Mounds of dirt around the entrances of these towns have an important job—they keep out floodwater. The mounds also make great watchtowers. Prairie dogs often sit on the mounds and watch for predators, such as foxes, coyotes, badgers, bobcats, eagles, hawks, and snakes.

When a prairie dog spots danger, it sounds the alarm—a chirp, a wheeze, and a flick of the tail. This lets other prairie dogs know that they should dive underground and hide.

A few prairie dogs wait in listening posts near the surface. When the danger is past, they carefully poke their heads out. Finally, one prairie dog gives the "all-clear" signal by throwing its head back and making a wheezy "yip." Soon all the prairie dogs are back aboveground eating grass and insects.

Old World Mice

FAMILY: Muridae

COMMON EXAMPLE: House mouse

GENUS AND SPECIES: *Mus musculus*

SIZE: 2 to 4 inches (5 to 10 cm);
2/5 to 4/5 ounces (11 to 23 g)

Who has been leaving little black pellets on the kitchen counter? Who has been shredding the dish towels in the drawer? Who has been gnawing on the dog biscuits in the cabinet? Chances are, the answer to all these questions is the same—a house mouse.

House mice came to North America (the New World) from Europe (the Old World) with the early settlers—hidden away in the holds of ships. Now they are found all over the continent. What is the secret of their success? They can live almost anywhere and eat almost anything.

They live in houses, barns, grassy fields, and even town dumps. In the wild, they eat caterpillars, beetle grubs, and other insects as well as all kinds of seeds. In houses, they eat cereals, bread, candy, meat, dog biscuits, and even the glue in book bindings.

In outdoor settings, house mice do more good than harm. They eat weed seeds and insects that destroy crops. But having a mouse in the house can be annoying. Mice get into all kinds of food packages, leave their droppings everywhere, and gnaw on furniture and woodwork.

Old World Rats

FAMILY: Muridae
COMMON EXAMPLE: Norway rat
GENUS AND SPECIES: *Rattus norvegicus*
SIZE: 12 to 18 inches (30 to 46 cm);
7 to 10 ounces (198 to 283 g)

Norway rats—also called brown rats—first came to North America (the New World) from Europe (the Old World) as stowaways during the Revolutionary War. Like house mice, they are now everywhere!

They live in sewers and subway tunnels, in grain fields, and in basements. As long as they have shelter and food, they grow and multiply quickly.

Norway rats will eat just about anything. They like grains, corn, fruit, and vegetables. They love eggs, chickens, and other small birds and animals. They are quite happy eating garbage, candy, or milk. They even eat soap!

These rats have such strong teeth that they can chew their way into cans and jelly jars. They like to gnaw on plaster, wood, and furniture. Sometimes they even gnaw on electrical wires.

Norway rats live in large "colonies" that may have more than fifty members. Each rat can identify other members of its colony by smell. The rats in a colony get along well with one another, but they will drive strange rats away in a hurry.

A female Norway rat can have as many as seventy babies a year. Each young rat is ready to have babies of its own when it is just 3 months old. No wonder rats have spread all over the world!

Deer Mice

FAMILY: Cricetidae
COMMON EXAMPLE: Deer mouse
GENUS AND SPECIES: *Peromyscus maniculatus*
SIZE: 4 to 9 inches (10 to 22 cm);
2/3 to 1 ounce (18 to 28 g)

A deer mouse has a reddish-brown back and a white belly. Its large ears and big, brown eyes may remind you of a deer.

Prairie deer mice live mostly in the midwestern United States. They nest in fields and feed on wheat, corn, and caterpillars. Woodland deer mice are bigger and live in wooded areas throughout the northeastern United States and Canada. They nest in burrows in the ground or in hollow logs and eat seeds, nuts, berries, insects, centipedes, and fungi. Other kinds of deer mice live in deserts and mountainous areas. Some even live in swamps.

Deer mice spend all summer getting ready for winter. They stuff their cheeks full of nuts and seeds, and carry the food to a storage place. These mice don't hibernate, so they must gather enough food in the warm months to get them through the winter.

Because deer mice only come out at night, you may never see one —unless a cat leaves one on your doorstep. But you may find one of their storage areas in a hollow log. If you look closely, you might see their tracks in fresh snow. They look like tiny rabbit tracks, but they have a little trail behind where the deer mouse dragged its long tail.

Chipmunks

FAMILY: Sciuridae

COMMON EXAMPLE: Eastern chipmunk

GENUS AND SPECIES: *Tamias striatus*

SIZE: 8 to 10 inches (20 to 25 cm);
2 to 5 ounces (56 to 141 g)

Who doesn't love to watch chipmunks scampering about as they collect nuts and seeds? Their striped coats and perky movements seem to charm everyone.

A busy chipmunk may stop suddenly and sit up on a stump, tail twitching. Then, it clasps its forepaws to its chest and starts to sing its "chip chip" song. Soon its neighbors join in, and the woods are filled with chipmunk chatter.

When a chipmunk spots an enemy, it lets out a sharp whistle and dives for cover. A chipmunk has many enemies—hawks, snakes, foxes, bobcats, and even house cats. Its worst enemy is the weasel. A skinny, sneaky weasel can follow a chipmunk right down into its burrow.

In the spring and early summer, chipmunks eat insects, slugs, birds' eggs, and even small birds. But what they like best are seeds, nuts, fruits, and berries. Have you ever seen a chipmunk's face stained with berry juice?

In late summer, chipmunks begin to gather nuts and seeds to store for the coming winter. They can carry as many as a dozen beechnuts in their cheeks. By the time winter comes, their storage rooms are full of food and the chipmunks are ready for the long cold months ahead.

Gray Squirrels

FAMILY: Sciuridae
COMMON EXAMPLE: Gray squirrel
GENUS AND SPECIES: *Sciurus carolinensis*
SIZE: 16 to 20 inches (40 to 51 cm);
15 to 25 ounces (425 to 708 g)

If you live in the eastern United States, you have probably seen more gray squirrels than any other wild mammal. They live in forests, suburbs, and city parks—anywhere they can find a supply of nuts and seeds.

Gray squirrels live and nest in trees. They like oak and beech trees best because acorns and beechnuts are their favorite foods. But in spring and early summer—before the nuts ripen—they eat plant buds, seeds, fruits and berries, and some insects. They may also eat birds' eggs or small birds.

In the fall, gray squirrels bury nuts and acorns to eat during the cold winter. They can't remember where they bury their nuts, so they rely on their good sense of smell to lead them to their food stashes. They can even smell nuts buried under a foot of snow.

Gray squirrels are great acrobats. They leap easily from tree to tree, hardly ever falling. Their bushy tails give them lift. If a gray squirrel does happen to fall, its fluttering tails acts like a parachute to slow it down. A squirrel may fall 30 feet (9 m), land with a thump, then get right up, and race back up the tree.

Red Squirrels

FAMILY: Sciuridae
COMMON EXAMPLE: Red squirrel
GENUS AND SPECIES: *Tamiasciurus hudsonicus*
SIZE: 11 to 14 inches (28 to 36 cm);
7 to 9 ounces (198 to 255 g)

A red squirrel is smaller than a gray squirrel, but it's not afraid of its bigger cousin. If a gray squirrel tries to steal a red squirrel's food, the red squirrel will chatter angrily to drive the rascal away.

Red squirrels are very quick and busy all the time. They only seem to rest during the worst winter storms. Red squirrels will eat almost anything that comes their way. In the spring and summer, they enjoy the same menu as gray squirrels. They also eat fungi.

When fall comes, they rush about gathering acorns, nuts, and seeds for the winter ahead. Red squirrels often cut off pine cones that are still green and bury them. They seem to know that if they wait until the pine cones are ripe and dry, the wind will blow away the seeds inside. They also store fungi in tree holes to dry.

Even in winter, red squirrels race around. They use their sense of smell to find buried nuts and seeds and scamper up and down trees searching for hidden stores of mushrooms.

When spring returns, these clever (and sweet-toothed) squirrels make slits in the trunks of maple trees, so they can nibble and suck on the sweet maple sap that flows out.

Flying Squirrels

FAMILY: Sciuridae
COMMON EXAMPLE: Southern flying squirrel
GENUS AND SPECIES: *Glaucomys volans*
SIZE: 8 to 10 inches (20 to 25 cm);
2 to 4 ounces (56 to 113 g)

Flying squirrels don't really fly, but they do glide from tree to tree. They have special folds of skin between their legs. When they leap from a tree, they spread out their legs. The folds of skin stretch out and act like a parachute. Flying squirrels can even change their direction and speed up or slow down as they glide.

Just before a flying squirrel lands, it drops its tail and pulls in the folds of skin. This action works like the brakes on a car. A flying squirrel can glide as far as 240 feet (73 m)!

At night, flying squirrels gorge on acorns, nuts, berries, insects, and birds' eggs. They may even catch and eat other small rodents. In the daytime, they hide in leafy nests in tree holes or, sometimes, in the attics of houses.

Red squirrels don't hibernate, but when it is very cold, they snuggle up with several other flying squirrels and snooze in their warm nests.

Gliding from tree to tree is a good way to escape their enemies. But flying squirrels still have to beware of hawks and owls—and house cats.

Porcupines

FAMILY: Erethizontidae

COMMON EXAMPLE: North American porcupine

GENUS AND SPECIES: *Erethizon dorsatum*

SIZE: 25 to 31 inches (64 to 79 cm);
10 to 28 pounds (4 to 13 kg)

Porcupines are slow, heavy rodents. They waddle about on the forest floor or climb slowly up tree trunks. Luckily, they don't have to worry too much about enemies. The long, sharp quills on their backs and tails have little barbs at the tips that hook into flesh. Nobody wants a mouthful of those quills!

If a dog comes nosing through the woods, spies a porcupine, and dashes in to attack, the porcupine will shake its quills to warn the dog away. If the silly dog attacks anyway, the porcupine will lower its head, raise its quills, and swing its tail right in the dog's face. The next thing the dog knows, it has a faceful of painful quills! The poor dog paws madly at its face to get them out, but the barbs at the end hold them fast.

A dog can run home so that its owners can pull the quills out. A wild animal isn't so lucky. Over time, the quills work deeper and deeper into the animal's skin. Quills in the animal's face may injure its eyes. Quills in its mouth may make eating difficult or impossible. That's why most predators leave porcupines alone.

A few predators—fishers and bobcats—may sneak up on a porcupine and flip the animal onto its back. Then they attack the porcupine's soft belly. The longest, sharpest quills in the world can't save a porcupine then!

Muskrats

FAMILY: Cricetidae

COMMON EXAMPLE: Muskrat

GENUS AND SPECIES: *Ondatra zibethica*

SIZE: 18 to 25 inches (46 to 64 cm);
2 to 4 pounds (1 to 2 kg)

You may have seen a muskrat swimming across a pond and thought it was a small beaver. If you looked closely, however, you would have seen that the animal's scaly tail was flattened vertically and that its front teeth were yellow. A beaver's tail is flattened horizontally, and its front teeth are orange.

Muskrats are well suited for life in marshes, ponds, and streams. They use their webbed back feet and their rudder-like tails to swim. They can close off the back of their mouths and gnaw on underwater plants. They can stay underwater for several minutes.

Muskrats build *lodges* to hide from their predators—hawks, owls, foxes, mink, and even humans! They pick a place where the water is shallow and make a platform of sticks and roots. Then they build a dome-shaped lodge on top with cattails and other water plants. Finally, they hollow out a room just above the water level and create one or two underwater entrances. Muskrats usually build smaller feeding platforms near the lodge. Their favorite foods include cattails, water lilies, and other water plants. A muskrat may also dine on fresh-water clams, crayfish, frogs, and dead fish.

Beavers

FAMILY: Castoridae
COMMON EXAMPLE: North American beaver
GENUS AND SPECIES: *Castor canadensis*
SIZE: 35 to 50 inches (89 to 127 cm);
30 to 60 pounds (14 to 27 kg)

Beavers are the largest rodents in North America. A 3-year-old beaver weighs about 30 pounds (14 kg). A beaver that manages to live until it is 16 years old may weigh 60 pounds (27 kg). A few beavers weigh as much as 100 pounds (45 kg)!

Beavers are even better suited than muskrats to life in the water. Beavers swim with their large, webbed back feet and use their broad tails as rudders. Their front paws are free to hold things.

A beaver can close off its ears, nose, and the back of its throat to keep water out. A clear film protects its eyes. Beavers produce a waterproofing oil, which they comb into their fur. A beaver's large lungs let it stay underwater for 15 minutes at a time!

Beavers are best known for their tree chopping and dam building. A beaver can chop down a 4-inch (10-cm)-thick tree in just 5 minutes!

Beavers can create a pond in the middle of a stream by building a dam from branches, mud, and stones. When the stream water backs up, the beaver builds a lodge in the middle of the new pond.

First, the beaver makes a large mound of more sticks and mud. Then it digs out underwater entrances and hollows out a den above the waterline. Inside the lodge, the beaver and its young are safe from enemies.

Rodents All Around

If you want to learn more about rodents, you can observe them in your backyard or a local park. They live in so many different habitats that it should be easy to find them.

Be sure to keep a rodent notebook. Write down everything the animals do and draw pictures that show their special features. Binoculars might also be helpful.

The easiest rodents to study are gray squirrels, red squirrels, and chipmunks. They are all active during the day and are fairly comfortable around people. You could probably collect enough information to write a book of your own!

You can look for other rodents, too. In the woods, keep an eye out for porcupines in the tree tops. They usually rest in trees during the day. In the early morning or evening, you may see them on the ground.

In a field, look for the tell-tale mounds of dirt around woodchuck burrows. If you see one, find a spot some distance away where you can see the woodchuck, but the woodchuck can't see you. Sooner or later the woodchuck will come out to eat.

In wetlands, look for muskrats' dome-shaped lodges. If you are close enough, you will smell their musky scent. Muskrats are most active in the evening and at night, but sometimes you can see them in the daytime. If you wait patiently—and out of sight, you may have a chance to watch a muskrat eating or working on its lodge.

Around ponds or streams, look for signs of beavers. You may be lucky enough to come across a beaver dam and lodge. If a beaver has

Beaver lodge

made a den in a riverbank, it may be difficult to spot. It might be easier to notice freshly gnawed and felled trees. These are signs that a beaver is nearby. Early morning and evening are the best times to watch for beavers, but you may see one in the middle of the day.

Other rodents may be harder to spot, but you can tell they're around by the signs they leave. Look for vole tunnels and holes in fields and gardens. Their trails are especially easy to see in early spring after the snow melts.

In the woods, you may find a heap of seeds in a hollow log. They were probably left by a deer mouse. You may also notice a deer mouse's rabbit-like tracks in the snow. If you find dried mushrooms stored in a tree hole, you can be pretty sure that a red squirrel put them there.

It's easy to tell if there are house mice living with you. You'll find their droppings on kitchen counters, shredded towels they have chewed to line their nests, and signs that they have been raiding the food cupboards. If your family tries to catch them with "hav-a-heart" traps, you might get a close-up look at a house mouse.

There are so many different kinds of rodents all over the world that you could spend your whole life studying them. Even then, you wouldn't have time to learn everything about them.

Rodents called capybara live in South America.

Words to Know

burrow—a shelter dug in the ground.

cheek teeth—the name given to a rodent's back teeth. They are used to chew food.

class—a group of creatures within a phylum that share certain characteristics.

family—a group of creatures within an order that share certain characteristics.

fungus (plural **fungi**)—one of the five kingdoms of living things. Fungi obtain nutrients from decaying plant and animal matter.

genus (plural **genera**)—a group of creatures within a family that share certain characteristics.

habitat—the environment where a plant or animal lives and grows.

hibernate—to spend the winter in a resting state, with a slowed heart rate and breathing.

incisor—a front tooth used for gnawing and cutting.

kingdom—one of the five divisions into which all living things are placed: the animal kingdom, the plant kingdom, the fungus kingdom, the moneran kingdom, and the protist kingdom.

lodge—a shelter built by muskrats or beavers.

litter—a group of baby mammals born at the same time to the same mother.

mammal—an animal that has a backbone and feeds its young with mother's milk.

order—a group of creatures within a class that share certain characteristics.

phylum (plural **phyla**)—a group of creatures within a kingdom that share certain characteristics.

predator—an animal that hunts and eats other animals.

rodent—an order of mammals with incisors that continue to grow throughout their lives.

species—a group of creatures within a genus that share certain characteristics. Members of a species can mate and produce young.

Learning More

Books

Bare, Colleen S. *Busy, Busy Squirrels*. New York: Dutton Children's Books, 1991.

George, William T. and Lindsay B. *Beaver at Long Pond*. New York: Greenwillow Books, 1988.

Hoffmeister, Donald and Zim, Herbert S. *Golden Guide to Mammals*. Racine, WI: Western Publishing Company, 1987.

Lepthien E. V. *Woodchucks*. Chicago: Children's Press, 1993.

Parsons, Alexandra. *Amazing Mammals*. New York: Knopf Books for Young Readers, 1990.

Videos

Rocky Mountain Beaver Pond. National Geographic Videos.

See How They Grow: Forest Animals. SONY Music Entertainment.

Web Sites

The Rodent Zone Page has general information about a wide variety of rodents.
http://members.tripod.com/~CloveApple/rodent.html

Rat and Mouse Club of America has a site that lists club activities, such as rodent shows, and interesting information about rats and mice.
http://www.rmca.org

Index

About the Author

Sara Swan Miller has enjoyed working with children all her life, first as a Montessori nursery school teacher, and later as an outdoor environmental educator at the Mohonk Preserve in New Paltz, New York. As the director of the Preserve school program, she has led hundreds of children on field trips and taught them the importance of appreciating and respecting the natural world, including mice, squirrels, beavers, and other rodents.

She has written a number of children's books including *Three Stories You Can Read to Your Dog*; *Three Stories You Can Read to Your Cat*; *What's in the Woods?: An Outdoor Activity Book*; *Oh, Cats of Camp Rabbitbone!*; *Piggy in the Parlor and Other Tales*; *Better Than TV*; and *Will You Sting Me? Will You Bite Me? The Truth About Some Scary-Looking Insects*.